THE BEST OF

Jane Grigson's
DESSERTS

Also by Jane Grigson

THE BEST OF
Jane Grigson's
DESSERTS

....

50 classic recipes

Jane Grigson

MICHAEL JOSEPH
LONDON

MICHAEL JOSEPH LTD
Published by the Penguin Group
27 Wrights Lane, London W8 5TZ
Viking Penguin Inc., 375 Hudson Street, New York, New York 10014, USA
Penguin Books Australia Ltd, Ringwood, Victoria, Australia
Penguin Books Canada Ltd, 10 Alcorn Avenue, Toronto, Ontario,
Canada M4V 3B2
Penguin Books (NZ) Ltd, 182–190 Wairau Road, Auckland 10, New Zealand
Penguin Books Ltd, Registered Offices: Harmondsworth, Middlesex, England

First published in Great Britain 1993
Copyright © Sophie Grigson 1993

Illustrations by Sarah McMenemy

Typeset by Selwood Systems, Midsomer Norton
Made and printed in England by Butler & Tanner Ltd, Frome and London
A CIP catalogue record for this book is available from the British Library

ISBN 0 7181 0043 3

The moral right of the author has been asserted

NOTE

The recipes in this book have been selected from Jane Grigson's many cookery books written over a number of years. Inevitably, therefore, the recipes vary in the amount of detailed method given and some assume knowledge of cooking techniques such as making pastry. If in doubt, an experienced cook will be able to use his/her own judgement; a less experienced cook will probably find enough assistance in any general cookery book.

....

QUANTITIES

Serving quantities are indicated at the beginning of each recipe, though these are intended as a general guide, and you must allow for the rest of the meal, or the position of a dish in the meal, when making your calculations.

When measuring ingredients, follow either metric or imperial systems, not a mixture. Metric measurements are given first.

PEAR TART

TARTE AUX POIRES

A beautiful recipe. Rich enough for an elegant dinner, simple enough to please the youngest child at Sunday lunch. To me, this is perfect food, with each good ingredient making its point in a pleasant harmony.

Serves 6

CREAMED PÂTÉ SUCRÉE
125 g (4 oz) soft butter
2 rounded tablespoons
 vanilla sugar
1 large egg
pinch salt
250 g (8 oz) plain flour

FILLING
4–5 ripe pears
1 tablespoon lemon juice
300 ml (10 fl oz) double
 or whipping cream
2 large egg yolks
vanilla sugar

First make the creamed pâte sucrée. Cream butter and sugar, add egg and salt. When the mixture is reasonably well amalgamated, add the flour. The dough should need no water. Chill it in the refrigerator for at least 30 minutes.

Roll out the chilled pastry and line a large tart tin, about 25 cm (10 in) in diameter, or slightly larger. Bake blind (page 11).

Meanwhile peel, core and slice the pears. This can be done longways or across, keeping the pear halves in shape. Sprinkle with lemon juice to prevent discolouring. Beat together the cream and egg yolks, sweetening to taste.

When the pastry comes out of the oven, arrange the pear slices on it. Long slices go in concentric circles; the sliced halves should be put on the pastry and spread out slightly so that they are flattened but still in the shape of the halves, with the pointed ends towards the centre. Pour over the cream mixture, and return to the oven. Close the door and turn the heat down to Gas mark 5, 190°C (375°F) until the cream is nearly firm. It tastes best when not quite set in the centre. Serve warm.

Note: apples can be used for this tart, eating apples. It is a good idea to cook the slices in a little butter first, so that they begin to soften. Should your pears be on the hard side, cook them gently in a little syrup with lemon juice and lemon zest.

BAKING BLIND: Line the tart tin with the pastry and prick the base with a fork. Leave to relax in the fridge for half an hour. Line with foil or greaseproof paper and weight down with baking beans. Bake blind at Gas mark 6, 200°C (400°F) for 10 minutes. Remove paper and beans and return to the oven for 5 minutes to dry out, without browning.

ANDALUSIAN TART

TARTE ANDALOUSE

The combination of aromatic eating apples with orange is remark-ably, surprisingly, successful. I tried the recipe with misgivings when I saw it in a French newspaper, but now it is a favourite of ours. Start by making a sweet shortcrust pastry (page 10), in which you have included the finely grated zest of a large orange (the orange will be needed later on for the filling). Let it rest, then line a tart tin of 23 cm (9 in) and bake it blind (page 11): it should be firm and creamy-coloured still, rather than brown.

Serves 6

500 g (1 lb) reinettes or Cox's or Blenheim Orange sugar

2 large oranges, seedless if possible
3 tablespoons apricot jam
juice of half a lemon

Peel, core and slice the apples. Boil peelings and cores in ¼ litre (8–9 fl oz) water to flavour it. Strain the water into a shallow pan – there should be about 125 ml (4 fl oz), but precision is not important; all that is needed is enough liquid to prevent the apples from burning as they cook.

Put the apple slices into the pan and cook them gently at first, turning the pieces. As they begin to soften, raise the heat to evaporate the juice as much as possible. Remove from the stove

when the apples are tender. Mash them well and sweeten to taste with about 75 g (2½ oz) sugar.

Meanwhile, peel the oranges to the quick with a sharp knife and slice them thinly, discarding any pips.

Spread the apple purée into the pastry case. Put the orange slices on top. Bake for about 15 minutes at Gas mark 6, 200°C (400°F), giving the fruit flavours a chance to blend, and the pastry time to brown nicely.

Have ready a thick apricot glaze made by boiling together the jam and lemon juice, then sieving it. Brush over the tart when you take it from the oven. Serve hot, warm (which is best) or cold.

PRUNE TART

A dish from Tours. For success, the prune purée must be rich and well-flavoured, not in the least watery.

Serves 6–8

250 g (8 oz) shortcrust pastry	*water*
500 g (1 lb) giant prunes, soaked	*sugar*
	rum
	beaten egg

Line a 23–25 cm (9–10 in) tart tin with a removable base with pastry (save the trimmings). Prick all over with a fork and bake blind until cooked, but not very brown (page 11).

Simmer the prunes in just enough water to cover them. Drain and sieve. Flavour the purée with sugar and rum, and put into the pastry case. Using the pastry trimmings, make a criss-cross lattice over it, with strips about 1 cm (¼ in) wide. Brush the pastry with beaten egg, and bake until golden brown (about 20 minutes at Gas Mark 6, 200°C (400°F)). Serve with cream.

Note: mix the prune purée above with double its weight in homemade vanilla ice-cream. Refreeze. Serve with almond biscuits. I know this sounds unpromising, but try it.

SHORTCRUST PASTRY

250 g (8 oz) plain flour　　*125 g (4 oz) butter*
pinch of salt　　　　　　　*1 egg*

Sift the flour with the salt. Rub in the butter. Add egg and enough iced water to make a soft dough. Knead briefly, then rest in the fridge for half an hour. Bring back to room temperature before using.

STRAWBERRY BRULÉE

Adapted from an American recipe, strawberry brulée sounds complicated, but it's really worth the trouble. You need a round, sightly, overproof dish (Pyrex is ideal) at least 2.5 cm (1 in) deep and about 20 cm (8 in) across.

Serves 6–8

SWEET SHORTCRUST
250g (8 oz) plain flour
2 tablespoons icing sugar
125g (4 oz) butter
1 egg

FILLING
300 ml (10 fl oz) single
   cream
150 ml (5 fl oz) double
   cream
3 egg yolks
15–20 large strawberries
1 tablespoon each orange
   liqueur and sugar
extra caster sugar

Make the pastry in the usual way (page 15) and line the Pyrex dish. Prick all over with a fork, and bake blind (page 11) until light brown and cooked.

Boil the cream, both kinds together, for one minute exactly. Stir into the egg yolks, beating with a fork. Set over a pan of simmering water for 5 minutes, stirring all the time to avoid lumps. Pour through a sieve into a clean basin and leave to cool.

Meanwhile halve the strawberries. Sprinkle with sugar and liqueur and set aside for an hour. Assemble the tart about 2½ hours before the meal. Arrange

the strawberries in a single close layer, flat side down on the pastry case. Mix their juice into the custard and pour over the fruit. Chill for 2 hours. Sprinkle the top with a bare 1 cm (¼ in) layer of caster sugar. Set under a hot grill, turning from time to time, so that the sugar melts into an even golden-brown marbled sheet of caramel. Chill for half an hour (while serving and eating the first course or courses).

PEACH AMBER

Originally, an amber pudding was a rich blend of butter and sugar set with egg yolks. The result was translucent and golden, hence the name. It was not until the turn of the nineteenth century that someone had the bright idea of supplementing the mixture with fruit and topping it with meringue. Peaches or nectarines are especially good.

Serves 6

*shortcrust pastry made
with 125 g (4 oz) plain
flour (page 15)*
*700 g (1½ lb) peaches,
skinned, stoned and
roughly chopped*
60 g (2 oz) unsalted butter
about 60 g (2 oz) sugar
*grated zest and juice of 1
lemon*

2 large egg yolks
*about 1 tablespoon cake
crumbs (optional)*
3 large egg whites
*a few drops of almond
essence*
*9 level tablespoons caster
sugar*
*angelica leaves and toasted
almonds to decorate*

Line a 20 cm (8 in) greased tart tin with the pastry, prick the base with a fork and put it into the fridge to chill. Heat the oven to Gas mark 5, 190°C (375°F) and put in a baking sheet to heat through.

Cook the peaches with the butter, sugar and lemon zest until they are tender. Cover until the juices run, then complete the cooking uncovered. Drain off and reserve the juice from the peaches. Mash the fruit to a purée, then put it through a sieve, using the reserved juice to help it through if need be. Stir in the egg yolks. If the purée is very sloppy, add a tablespoon of cake crumbs. Taste, and add more lemon juice or sugar. Spread the peach amber into the pastry case and put it on top of the hot baking sheet. After 20 minutes in the oven, check to see if the filling has set. Be prepared to leave it for a further 5–10 minutes. Remove the tart and lower the oven temperature to Gas mark 2, 150°C (300°F).

Whisk the egg whites until they stand in stiff peaks. Beat in a few drops of essence and half the caster sugar, beating after each spoonful is added. Fold in the remaining sugar quickly and lightly with a metal spoon. Pile this meringue on to the tart, spreading it right to the edges. Decorate with small leaves of angelica and toasted almonds. Put it into the oven and leave until evenly browned – about 20 minutes. Serve warm, with cream if you like, though personally, I prefer it without.

YORKSHIRE CURD TART

Serves 6

250 g (8 oz) weight
  shortcrust pastry (page
  15), made with lard and
  sour milk

FILLING
125 g (4 oz) butter
60 g (2 oz) sugar
250 g (8 oz) curd cheese
  (not cottage or cream
  cheese)
125 g (4 oz) seedless
  raisins, or currants
1 rounded tablespoon
  wholemeal breadcrumbs
pinch salt
grated nutmeg to taste
2 well-beaten eggs

Line a 20–25 cm (8–10 in) tart tin with the pastry – use the kind with a removable base. Cream the butter and sugar together, mix in the curds, raisins or currants and breadcrumbs. Add the salt and nutmeg and lastly the eggs. Taste and adjust nutmeg, add a little more sugar if you like (I find most recipes too sweet). Pour into the pastry case and bake for 20–30 minutes at Gas mark 7, 220°C (425°F). The pastry should be a nice brown.

BAKEWELL TART

Commercially-produced Bakewell tarts often contain ground almonds which is quite wrong. The real filling is a rich custard of butter and eggs, which is closer to the *mirliton* tarts made at Rouen (page 25) than to English almond tarts. This recipe was a speciality of the inn at Bakewell when Jane Austen stayed (do you remember Mr Darcy's estate at Pemberley in Derbyshire, where Elizabeth Bennet began to realize her love for him?)

Serves 6

250 g (8 oz) weight rich shortcrust pastry (page 15)

FILLING
*strawberry jam
125 g (4 oz) butter
125 g (4 oz) sugar
4 egg yolks
3 egg whites*

Roll out the pastry and line one large tart tin or several small patty pans. Spread the pastry with jam.

Melt the butter (the flavour will be even more delicious if you allow it to cook to a golden brown), then mix it boiling hot with the sugar and egg yolks and whites which have been beaten together in a bowl. Put this mixture over the pastry. Bake at Gas mark 6–7, 200–220°C (400–425°F), for 20–30 minutes until lightly browned. Eat immediately.

SWEETMEAT CAKE

This delicious cake with its butterscotch flavour and semi-transparent filling is my own favourite of the eighteenth-century open tarts. Candied peel provides the 'sweetmeat': it can be augmented with angelica, and the hazelnuts mentioned, but don't be tempted to add glacé cherries as they spoil the subtle flavour.

Serves 6

225 g (9 oz) puff or
 shortcrust pastry (page
 15)
125 g (4 oz) chopped peel
60 g (2 oz) chopped roasted
 hazelnuts (optional)

2 large eggs
2 large egg yolks
175 g (6 oz) caster sugar
175 g (6 oz) lightly salted
 butter, melted

Line a 23 cm (9 in) flan tin with the pastry. Scatter the chopped peel over it, then the hazelnuts if used. Beat the remaining ingredients thoroughly together and pour the mixture over the peel. Bake at Gas mark 4, 180°C (350°F), for 35–40 minutes. The top should be crusted with a rich golden brown all over – so keep an eye on it after 30 minutes in the oven. At first the filling will rise with the baking, but once the cake is removed from the oven and transferred to a plate, it will sink again as these egg mixtures usually do. Do not worry if the centre part of the filling is a little liquid beneath the crust, as it makes a delicious sauce. The consistency is a matter for individual taste. Like most sweet tarts, this is best eaten warm. Serve with cream.

> *Note:* This recipe is a forerunner of the nursery favourite, treacle tart, but it has a much superior flavour. Treacle tart is filled with a mixture of 3 tablespoons golden syrup, 3 tablespoons white breadcrumbs and the grated rind of a lemon: bake it at Gas mark 7, 220°C (425°F), for 20–30 minutes.

JEFFERSON DAVIS TART

Jefferson Davis was head of the Confederacy of the Southern States of America, until defeat in 1865 by the North at the end of the Civil War. It seems inappropriate that anyone who shared in that experience of carnage should have a sweet frothy-topped tart named after him. For me, the tart is improved by using all dates, rather than half dates, half raisins, and I halve the quantity of sugar to the amount listed below. A good pudding for a family lunch party.

Serves 6

125 g (4 oz) softened butter
150 g (5 oz) light brown sugar
3 large egg yolks
250 ml (8 fl oz) whipping cream
1 level teaspoon cinnamon
½ teaspoon allspice
⅓ nutmeg, finely grated
6–8 stoned, chopped dates
100 g (3½ oz) raisins
60 g (2 oz) roughly broken pecans, or walnuts
MERINGUE
3 large egg whites
125 g (4 oz) caster sugar

Line a 23 cm (9 in) tart tin with 250 g (8 oz) plain shortcrust pastry (page 15). Mix together the ingredients in the order given. Bake at Gas mark 6, 200°C (400°F) for 10–15 minutes, then down to Gas mark 3, 160°C (325°F) for a further 20 minutes. Whisk the egg whites, and sweeten them with the caster sugar, to make a meringue. Spread over the top of the tart, and put back into the oven until nicely browned (about 20 minutes).

MIRLITONS DE ROUEN

Mirliton is a nonsense word from the refrain of old songs; it suggests a cheerful twirling of skirts and light feet and suits these tarts well.

Makes about 12

450 g (1 lb) puff pastry
4 egg yolks
50 g (2 oz) caster sugar
1 vanilla pod

125 g (4 oz) butter, plus
extra for greasing
1–2 teaspoons orange-
flower water or orange
liqueur

Preheat the oven. Roll out the pastry and line twelve greased tartlet tins. Put them into the refrigerator to chill for half an hour at least.

Beat together the yolks and nearly all the sugar, keeping 1 tablespoon back, until the mixture is pale and thick. Slit the vanilla pod and scrape the soft black seedy pulp into the egg and sugar. Mix well.

Cut up the butter, melt it in a small pan and cook it to a golden-brown colour; it should have an appetizing smell of nuts. Mix it vigorously into the egg yolks and flavour it to taste with orange-flower water, adding this ½ teaspoon at a time (it is much stronger than you might think). An orange liqueur does not taste at all the same, but it gives a slight zip to the mixture.

Fill the tartlet cases two-thirds full. Sprinkle them with the remaining sugar. Bake them in the oven for 10–15 minutes at Gas mark 7, 220°C (425°F); they may sink a little.

DUCLAIR CHERRY TART

TARTE AUX CERISES DE DUCLAIR

Duclair is on the Seine upstream from Tancarville, not far from Rouen. Ducks are a speciality; so is this unusual cherry tart. The tricky bit is cooking the cherries so that they caramelize without becoming over-cooked: you need a high heat once the butter, sugar and Calvados are blended, but take care the cherry juices do not burn – this kind of thing is much easier to do on a gas burner than an electric ring.

You need a puff pastry case, baked blind in a 23–25 cm (9–10 in) tart tin. This can be done in advance, and the case reheated to freshen it if necessary. The cream and cheese can also be mixed earlier in the day. But the cooking of the cherries and the final assembly should take place not too long before the meal.

Serves 6

*500 g (1 lb) firm red
cherries, stoned weight*
60 g (2 oz) butter
*100 g (3½ oz) granulated
sugar*
*3 tablespoons Calvados or
malt whisky*

*250 g (8 oz) fromage frais
caster sugar*
*150 ml (5 fl oz) double
cream*

Drain the cherries in a sieve. Melt the butter, stir in the granulated sugar and Calvados, or whisky. When they are blended, raise the heat and put in the cherries. They should caramelize lightly, so keep them moving and do not take your eye off them. Drain and cool.

Beat the *fromage frais* with caster sugar to taste. Whip the cream and fold it in, check again for sweetness and taste a cherry to make sure that you do not over-sweeten the mixture.

To assemble, spread the cream cheese and cream on to the pastry. Put the cherries on top.

ROBERT SOUTHEY'S GOOSEBERRY PIE

Do you follow the country tradition of eating the first gooseberry pie of the season at Whitsunday lunch? If you do, here's a nice proposition of Robert Southey's to stimulate quiet post prandial reflection: 'Two gooseberry pies being supposed, their paste made at the same time, and indeed of one mass, the gooseberries gathered from the same bushes and of equal age, the sugar in just proportion, and clotted cream to eat with both, it follows that the largest is preferable. I love gooseberry pie ... I think the case is plain.'

Serves 6–8

30 g (1 oz) butter
250 g (8 oz) shortcrust
* pastry (page 15)*
1 kg (2 lb) gooseberries,
* young and green*

175–250 g (6–8 oz)
* sugar*
1 egg white

Grease a 1 litre (2 pt) pie dish with the butter. Roll out the pastry; moisten the edges of the pie dish and fasten a strip of pastry round it. Top and tail the gooseberries, put them into the dish with sugar between the layers (very sharp gooseberries will need 250g (8 oz)) and mound them up in the centre above the rim. Brush the pastry edge with egg white before laying on the pastry lid; knock up the edges, brush with egg white and sprinkle it with an even layer of caster sugar. Bake at Gas mark 6, 200°C (400°F), for 30–40 minutes. Serve with cream.

PLUM AND WALNUT PIE

A most delicious pie, with walnuts, cinnamon and butter to counteract the fruit's acidity. Choose a mild plum: the Quetsche or Zwetschke is ideal.

Serves 6

450 g (1 lb) (page 15) shortcrust pastry
500 g (1 lb) plums, halved, stoned, chopped
125 g (4 oz) soft light brown or demerara sugar
125 g (4 oz) chopped walnuts

2 teaspoons ground cinnamon
grated rind of ½ lemon and ½ orange
60 g (2 oz) melted butter
beaten egg or top of the milk to glaze

Line a 20–23 cm (8–9 in) pie dish about 2.5 cm (1 in) deep with pastry. Mix plums, sugar, walnuts, cinnamon and grated rinds and put into the pastry. Pour over the butter. Cover with pastry, pinching the edges and making a central hole. Brush over with beaten egg or top of the milk. Bake at Gas mark 5, 190°C (375°F) for about an hour. Serve warm with cream.

> *Note:* This pie can also be made with greengages, almonds and white sugar.

BANANA DUMPLINGS

This way of cooking bananas brings out their quality of aromatic richness that remains hidden and unsuspected in the huge bananas of modern commerce when eaten raw. Puff, flaky or shortcrust pastry are all suitable but I prefer the lightness of the first two: the quantity given below is the final weight, not the weight of the flour. Use just ripe bananas that are firm enough to handle easily.

Serves 6

6 bananas
2 heaped tablespoons sugar
2 heaped teaspoons
  cinnamon
750 g (1½ lb) pastry
beaten egg or light cream
  to glaze

Peel the bananas and roll them in sugar mixed with the cinnamon, spooning it over the inside surface of any curve so that the whole of the fruit is lightly coated.

Cut the pastry into six equal pieces. Roll out the first one into a rectangle and enclose the banana. The easiest way to do this, I find, is to place the banana on the pastry diagonally, then flip a corner over the curved centre part, and roll the banana in the pastry croissant-style. Brush the edges with water and press them firmly together. Make a few slits in the top of the pastry, and lay the whole thing on a baking sheet that has either been lightly greased (shortcrust) or moistened (flaky, puff). Brush over with egg or cream. Repeat with the remaining bananas and pastry. You will have quite a number of pastry trimmings left over by the time you have cut away the surplus thicknesses and odd unnecessary corners: if you are skilful with your fingers, you may find that you can manage with less pastry than I have stipulated above.

Bake at Gas mark 7, 220°C (425°F) for 15 minutes, or until nicely browned. With shortcrust pastry, you may like to lower the heat to Gas mark 5, 190°C (375°F) at this point. These dumplings need far less time than apple dumplings since bananas cook fast.

STRAWBERRY FRITTERS

BEIGNETS AUX FRAISES

One evening in Paris, we went to the Escargot restaurant in the rue Montorgeuil, in search of snails of course, and of Montreuil peaches. I did not expect to find anything special about the strawberry fritters which I chose out of curiosity for dessert. It had been a good meal, in black and red surroundings of past elegance, with a close friend. Those fritters were to be the fault, the way Chinese and Japanese potters deliberately put a fault into their vases to make them human. But I was not allowed my fault after all. The fritters were perfection, the batter crisp, the strawberry inside firm but meltingly delicious. Even the *crème anglaise* was right.

The Escargot fritters, half a dozen, were served in the centre of a large plate with a thin custard covering the base. A good combination, so long as you make the custard of eggs and milk, or milk and cream. Pour it on to each plate and leave in a cool place.

FOR EACH PERSON
6 fine strawberries, hulled

BATTER
125 g (4 oz) plain flour
¼ teaspoon salt
grated peel of ½ a lemon
1 tablespoon white wine
2 eggs, separated
water
1 tablespoon oil

Make a batter by mixing flour, salt, grated lemon peel, wine and egg yolks and enough water to make a single cream consistency. Just before cooking the fritters, stir in the oil and 2 egg whites stiffly beaten.

Spear the hulled strawberries, one by one, with a skewer, or two-pronged fork. Dip into the batter and then into deep-frying clean oil, preheated to 195°C (385°F). Cook about six at a time. You can keep them warm in the oven, but it is better to serve people straight from the pan even if they do have to eat seriatim. That way, the batter stays crisp.

EMPEROR'S PANCAKE

KAISERSCHMARRN

A fluffy pancake inspired by Emperor Franz Joseph I and a great Viennese speciality. If you prefer, you can bake the pancake in the oven at Gas mark 6, 200°C (400°F).

Serves 4

200 g (7 oz) plain flour
pinch of salt
60 g (2 oz) caster sugar
4 large egg yolks
3 tablespoons butter, melted
60 g (2 oz) sultanas

scant 500 ml (good 15 fl oz) milk
4 large egg whites
a little butter
extra caster sugar

Mix the first six ingredients, then beat in the milk. Whisk the whites stiffly and fold them in. Melt butter in two pans. Divide the mixture between them – it should be about 2 cm (¾ in) thick. When golden brown, turn and cook on the other side.

Pull apart with two forks in the pan, making rough little pieces and cook briefly, turning them about. Divide between four hot plates and sprinkle with sugar. Serve immediately with *Zwetschkenröster*:

ZWETSCHKENRÖSTER

*1 kg (2 lb) Zwetschke
(Quetsche) plums, or other
dark plums
150 g (5 oz) sugar*

*2 cloves
small cinnamon stick
juice and rind of 1 lemon*

Zwetschke plums can be gently torn apart and the stone picked out; other varieties may need more effort.

Simmer remaining ingredients with 125 ml (4 fl oz) water for 5 minutes, then put in the plum halves and stir until thick. The plums should fall into lumpy pieces, the final result being somewhere between a compote and a jam. This mixture can be used for fruit dumplings.

Do not give up hope of finding Zwetschke plums in England. I heard of some in Cambridge market two years ago and the friend who bought them wrote to me that 'Austrians do not think of it as just another plum – like Kraur (smooth cabbage) and Kohl (crinkly cabbage), there is the Pflaume (plum) and the Zwetschke.'

BLUEBERRY AND APPLE CRISP

In America, blueberries have been declared 'the aristocrat of soft fruit' – with some justification, too, whether we use them fresh, frozen, or canned. Our wild European bilberries are fine, but these North American relatives are bigger, sweeter and more succulent, and are frozen and canned by the ton. They characterize the blueberry barrens; but they are also cultivated in various forms. So are 'highbush' blueberries, fruit of *Vaccinium corymbosum*, which are easier to harvest from their tall heavy-cropping plants. It is these highbush blueberries which a few English growers are raising now in Dorset and Devon.

The addition of apple, sour apple, in this recipe gives an extra edge to the blueberries, without being identifiable. It melts into the purple fruit. The superior crumble mixture is so good that it is worth using with other fruit: pecans are difficult to find at other times of the year than Christmas, but walnuts, almonds or hazelnuts – whichever is best suited to the fruit – can take their place.

Serves 6

300–325 g (10–11 oz)
blueberries
250 g (8 oz) peeled, sliced
cooking apples
juice and grated rind of a
lemon
175 g (6 oz) soft brown
sugar

TOPPING
150 g (5 oz) plain flour
125 g (4 oz) granulated
sugar
1 level teaspoon baking
powder
¾ level teaspoon salt
50 g (1½ oz) butter
1 large egg, lightly beaten
8 pecan nuts or walnuts,
shelled and chopped
½ teaspoon cinnamon

Mix the blueberries and apples with the lemon rind and juice and the brown sugar. Spread out in a gratin dish of 1½ litre (2½ pt) capacity, which has been lightly buttered.

Mix the first four topping ingredients, rub in the butter, then add egg and nuts. Spread over the fruit. Sprinkle cinnamon over the whole thing and put into a hot oven, Gas mark 6, 200°C (400°F) for half an hour or until the top is nicely browned and the apples are soft. If the top browns too fast, lower the temperature. Serve hot with cream, or vanilla ice cream.

APRICOT AND ALMOND CRUMBLE

An elegant version of the homely crumble. It is always a great success with our French and Italian friends, who ask for an English pudding but whose pioneering spirit would fail if faced with Spotted Dick or Dead Man's Leg.

Serves 6

24 large apricots
sugar
60 g (2 oz) blanched,
  slivered almonds

CRUMBLE
125 g (4 oz) plain flour
125 g (4 oz) caster sugar
125 g (4 oz) ground
  almonds
175 g (6 oz) butter

Peel and quarter apricots (if the skins are in good condition and not tough, you need not bother with the peeling). Arrange them in a shallow baking dish. Sprinkle with sugar. Mix dry crumble ingredients together, then rub in butter. Spread over fruit. Top with the slivered almonds. Bake at Gas mark 6, 200°C (400°F) until the top is nicely coloured – about 35 minutes. If you find the top colouring too rapidly, lower the heat to Gas mark 4, 180°C (350°F). Serve hot or warm, with cream or custard sauce.

SEVILLE ORANGE PUDDING

A version of those delicious sponge puddings with a rich sauce underneath.

Serves 6–8

85 g (3 oz) butter, softened
230 g (8 oz) caster sugar
grated zest and juice of 3
*   Seville oranges*

5 large eggs, separated
60 g (2 oz) flour, sifted
280 ml (½ pt) milk

Preheat the oven to Gas mark 4, 180°C (350°F). Grease a soufflé dish with butter paper.

Put the butter into a processor and cream it, gradually adding the sugar. When pale and fluffy, add the orange zest, then the juice, then the yolks one by one. The mixture may curdle – this doesn't matter. Beat in the flour, alternating with tablespoons of milk. Whisk the egg whites until stiff. Fold in the orange mixture. Put into the dish and stand on a rack in a roasting pan. Pour in very hot water to come half way up the side of the dish. Put into the oven for around 50 minutes, or until nicely browned and firm on top. Serve warm.

RED CURRANT TART

RIBISELKUCHON

A strength of Austrian cake making is the succession of shortcakes, each slightly different, all deliciously crisp and rich. Traunkirchner torte, Linzertorte and this tart are only three out of a magnificent choice. If red currants are not in season, or available frozen, use raspberries or slightly sharp cherries instead.

Serves 8–10

160 g (5½ oz) softened butter
160 g (5½ oz(caster sugar
4 large egg yolks
100 g (3½ oz) ground almonds
300 g (10 oz) plain flour

FRUIT
about 500 g (1 lb) red currants
4 large egg whites
200 g (7 oz) caster sugar

Cream butter and sugar, add yolks and dry ingredients to make a heavy crumbly dough. Or mix in the processor all together. Spread evenly into a 22 cm (9 in) tart or shallow cake tin, preferably one with a removable base. Bake 30 minutes at Gas mark 5, 190°C (375°F). Check after 20 minutes and lower the heat if the edges have begun to brown.

Meanwhile, shred red currants from their stalks and leaves (use a fork). Some Austrian recipes instruct you to cook them

lightly, others leave them raw, which I prefer; the advantage of cooking them is that you can control the liquid content by reducing it – in wet summers the uncooked fruit may be so juicy that it overflows the tart. Whisk egg whites stiff, add half the sugar. Whisk again, then add the rest of the sugar.

Take the cake from the oven and turn heat to Gas mark 5, 190°C (375°F). Spread fruit over the cake, leaving a clear rim. Pile on the meringue to the edge of the tin, and put cake into the hot oven for about 15 minutes. Or until the top is nicely caught with brown. Cool and cut into small pieces to serve.

PINEAPPLE UPSIDE-DOWN PUDDING (CAKE)

A splendid pudding when made with fresh pineapple, which lifts it right out of the second class. Resist the temptation to stick glacé cherries into the holes of the pineapple slices: lightly toasted hazelnuts rubbed free of skin are more harmonious. I agree that you need something to bring the final appearance up to the taste.

Serves 6–8

one large pineapple *60 g (2 oz) butter*
60g (2 oz) hazelnuts *60 g (2 oz) sugar*

For 6–8 people, I use an oval gratin dish of 2 litre (4 pt) capacity, measuring 35 × 25 cm (14 × 10 in). It takes a large pineapple, peeled and not too thickly cut, to cover it. Remove the central core from the slices and halve all except three slices to go in the centre. Toast the hazelnuts in the oven that you have switched on to heat up for the pudding. Rub off their skins.

Into the base of the gratin dish pour the butter and sugar that you have melted together. Brush the mixture up the sides, then let it fall back. Put the pineapple slices on the base, with the hazelnuts in the holes and gaps. Now mix together with an electric beater or processor the following ingredients:

250 g (8 oz) soft butter
4 large eggs
250 g (8 oz) sugar
200 g (6 oz) self-raising
 flour
2 level teaspoons baking
 powder

50 g (2 oz) ground
 hazelnuts, or hazelnuts
 and almonds mixed
liquid left from cutting up
 pineapple

When smooth, spread over the pineapple evenly. Bake at Gas mark 4, 180°C (350°F) for about 50 minutes, or until cooked – if you use a deeper dish than mine, it will take longer. The top should be a beautiful golden brown. Run a knife blade round the edge of the pudding and turn it out on to a hot dish. If any

nuts have moved out of place, put them back where you can and don't worry about the rest. Absolute precision is not always appetizing.

Serve hot, warm or cold. Cream or soft chilled *coeur à la crème* go well with the hot pudding. Cold, as cake, it needs nothing with it.

STEAMED GINGER PUDDING

Serves 4

90 g (3 oz) butter
90 g (3 oz) caster sugar
1 large or 2 small eggs
125 g (4 oz) self-raising
  flour
125 g (4 oz) preserved
  ginger, chopped
1 tablespoon ginger syrup

¼ teaspoonful ground
  ginger
scant 150 ml (5 fl oz) milk

Cream butter and sugar until light, add the egg(s), then the flour, ginger, syrup and ground ginger. Mix to a soft cake dough with the milk. Put into a pudding basin leaving plenty of room for the pudding to rise. Cover and steam (see page 46) for 2 hours. Turn out and serve with a thin egg custard sauce, or with the following wine sauce:

WINE SAUCE

2 yolks of eggs
half a tablespoon sugar

150 ml (5 fl oz) sherry
90 g (3 oz) cream

Put the yolks, sugar and sherry into a basin. Whisk them together, then stand the basin over a pan of just simmering water. Continue to whisk until it thickens, adding the cream gradually. It should be light and frothy. The snag with this kind of sauce is that it should be served immediately it is made – which leaves rather a gap in the meal. On the other hand, it is a sauce worth waiting for.

Note: Homelier versions of this pudding use 1 teaspoonful of ground ginger and 1 tablespoonful of golden syrup as a substitute for the preserved ginger and ginger syrup.

SUSSEX POND PUDDING

The best of all English boiled suet puddings. In the middle the butter and sugar melt to a rich sauce, which is sharpened with the juice from the lemon. The genius of the pudding is the lemon. Its citrus bitter flavour is a subtlety which raises the pudding to the highest class. When you serve it, make sure that everyone has a piece of lemon, which will be much softened by the cooking, but still vigorous.

The name of the pudding refers to the sauce, which runs out of it, when it is turned on to a serving dish, and provides it with a moat of buttery brown liquid.

Serves 4–6

250 g (8 oz) self-raising flour
125 g (4 oz) chopped fresh beef suet
125 g (4 oz) slightly salted butter

milk and water
125 g (4 oz) Demerara sugar
1 large lemon, or 2 limes

Mix the flour and suet together in a bowl. Make into a dough with milk and water, half and half; 150 ml (5 fl oz) should be plenty. The dough should be soft, but not too soft to roll out into a large circle. Cut a quarter out of this circle, to be used later as the lid of the pudding. Butter a pudding basin lavishly. It should contain about 1½ litres (2½ pt). Drop the three-quarter circle of pastry into it and press the cut sides together to make a perfect join. Put half the butter, cut up, into the pastry, with half the sugar. Prick the lemon (or limes) all over with a larding needle, so that the juices will be able to escape, then put it (them) on to the butter and sugar. Add the remaining butter, cut in pieces, and sugar. Roll out the pastry which was set aside to make a lid. Lay it on top of the filling, and press the edges together so that the pudding is sealed in completely. Put a piece of foil right over the basin, with a pleat in the middle. Tie it in place with string, and make a string handle over the top so that the pudding can be lifted about easily. Put a large pan of water on to boil, and lower the pudding into it; the water must be boiling, and it should come halfway, or a little further, up the basin. Cover and leave to boil for 3–4 hours. If the water gets low, replenish it with *boiling* water. To serve, put a deep dish over the basin after removing the foil lid, and quickly turn the whole thing upside down: it is a good idea to ease the pudding from the sides of the basin with a knife first. Put on the table immediately.

SUMMER PUDDING IN THE
FLORENTINE STYLE

If some national opinion poll decided to find out our favourite pudding, many people would, I think, reply, 'Oh, summer pudding – with plenty of cream.' And whether filled with black currants, or with raspberries and red currants, it is indeed one of the most delectable things imaginable – so long as it's made with proper bread. If sliced bread happens to be your doom, use sponge cake instead.

I chose this pudding in the Otello restaurant in Florence, because I was intrigued by the tracery of brown lines, which made it look like a phrenologist's model head.

Serves 6

*1 large sponge cake of the
Victoria or Genoese type
375 g (12 oz) raspberries
100–125 g (3½–4 oz)
icing sugar*

*2–3 tablespoons orange
liqueur or kirsch
250 ml (8 fl oz) double
cream
4 tablespoons single cream*

Slice the top from the sponge cake fairly thinly, and set it aside. Cut the rest of the cake into three layers, and use them to line a large pudding basin, cutting the pieces to fit as irregularly as you like, and pushing them closely together. The brown edges of the cake will form the irregular pattern of brown lines I was talking about.

Sprinkle the raspberries with the sugar. Leave for an hour or two until they are bathed in a certain amount of juice – about 150 ml (5 fl oz). Strain off the juice, mix it with the liqueur or kirsch, and use it to moisten the sponge lining: stop before it becomes too wet.

Whip the creams until thick and standing in peaks. Fold in the raspberries and fill the sponge-lined basin. Put the top of the cake on as a lid, trimming it to fit if necessary. Place a plate inside the rim of the basin, and leave overnight. Next day, remove the plate, and invert a serving dish on top. Turn the whole thing upside down to serve. The sponge cake will have acquired a pinkish look. No extra cream is required for serving; if some of the filling is left over, spoon it round the base of the pudding.

POOR KNIGHT'S PUDDING WITH
RASPBERRIES

Before the last war, when tea was an occasion for enjoyment and not for guilt, we often used to have home-made raspberry jam sandwiches at my grandmother's house. There were always too many – raspberry jam being her favourite – and the next day they would appear as a pudding, having been fried in butter. I always thought, and still do think, that their latter end was more glorious than their debut. This recipe is my adaptation of her economy. It works well, too, with really ripe apricots and peaches. In winter one can use a really good jam, but I find this too sweet.

Serves 6–8

500 g (1 lb) raspberries
125 g (¼ lb) icing sugar
cinnamon
8 slices white bread
175 g (6 oz) butter
175 g (6 fl oz) whipping
cream, or 90 g (3 fl oz)
each double and single
cream
1 heaped tablespoon
caster sugar

Sprinkle raspberries with the icing sugar and about half a teaspoon of cinnamon. Leave until they produce some liquid and look like a slightly runny wholefruit jam. Taste and add more cinnamon and sugar if necessary.

Cut the crusts off the bread. Bring the butter to the boil in a small pan, then pour it, through a muslin-lined sieve, into a frying pan; fry the bread in it. This sounds laborious, but it is quickly done, and avoids the risk of the bread browning too much — it should look golden, and be crisp.

Keep the bread warm in the oven, while you whip the creams together and sweeten them to taste with the sugar. Sandwich the bread with raspberries, and top with a generous swirl of whipped cream. You have a delicious contrast between the keen, buttery heat of the bread, and the keen cold of the raspberries, softened by the cream.

QUEEN OF PUDDINGS

A pudding which deserves its name for the perfect combination of flavours and textures, a most subtle and lovely way to end a meal.

Serves 4–6

150g (5 oz) fresh brown or
    white breadcrumbs
1 heaped tablespoon
    vanilla sugar
grated rind of 1 large
    lemon
600 ml (20 fl oz) milk
60g (2 oz) lightly salted
    butter

4 large egg yolks
2 tablespoons blackcurrant
    jelly, or raspberry jelly
4 large egg whites
125 g (4 oz) caster sugar,
    plus 1 extra teaspoonful

Put breadcrumbs, vanilla, sugar and lemon rind into a pudding basin. Bring the milk and butter to just below boiling point and stir it into the crumbs. Leave for 10 minutes, then beat in the egg yolks thoroughly. Grease a shallow dish which holds about 1½ litres (2½ pt) with a buttery paper, and pour in the bread-crumb custard. Bake at Gas mark 4, 180°C (350°F), for 30 minutes, or a little less, until just firm – the time will depend on the depth of the dish, and remember that the custard will continue to cook a little in its own heat so that if the centre looks runny underneath the skin do not feel anxious. Warm the jelly (if you use jam, warm it and sieve it) and spread it over the custard without breaking the surface. Whisk the whites until stiff, mix in half the caster sugar, then whisk again until slightly satiny. With a metal spoon, fold in the rest of the sugar. Pile on to the pudding, sprinkle with the extra teaspoonful of sugar and return to the oven for 15 minutes until the meringue is slightly browned and crisp. Serve hot with plenty of cream.

LEMON RICE PUDDING

This beautiful lemon pudding is based on the Portuguese *Arroz Doce*, sweet rice. Guaranteed to convert the most ardent rice-pudding-hater.

Serves 6

45 g (1½ oz) rice
1 lemon
30 g (1 oz) sugar
30 g (1 oz) butter

300 ml (10 fl oz) creamy milk and 300 ml (10 fl oz) single cream or 600 ml (20 fl oz) single cream
cinnamon
extra cream

Wash the rice, and peel the lemon thinly, taking off strips about 1 cm (¼ in) wide and 2.5 cm (1–2 in) long. Put rice, lemon peel, sugar, butter and single cream and milk into a pyrex or other ovenproof dish. Cook in a very slow oven, Gas mark ½, 135°C (250°F), for 2 to 3 hours until the rice is cooked. Stir it every three quarters of an hour. About half an hour before the pudding is cooked, add about a teaspoon of cinnamon or less, depending on your taste. When the pudding is done, stir it up well, adding the lemon juice and some more cream if it's too solid. Put a light sprinkling of cinnamon on top and place under a medium hot grill to brown the top lightly. Serve well chilled. You will find that the lemon peel has almost dissolved, and so has the rice although it still feels gently grainy to the tongue.

ANGEL'S HAIR CHARLOTTE

CHARLOTTE AUX CHEVEUX D'ANGE

Serves 6

250 g (8 oz) medium grated carrots
250 g (8 oz) sugar
peel and juice of a large lemon
32 boudoir biscuits

juice of a large orange
125 ml (4 fl oz) each double and single cream, or 250 ml (8 fl oz) whipping cream
60 g (2 oz) split, toasted almonds

Put the carrots, sugar, lemon peel cut in strips, lemon juice and 150 ml (¼ pt) water into a pan. Heat slowly until the sugar is dissolved, then bring to the boil and cook hard until the mixture is jammy and thick.

Line a charlotte mould with foil. Dip the biscuits briefly into orange juice and arrange them, sugar side out, round the walls of the mould. Fit more biscuits, cut to shape, in the bottom.

Whip the cream(s) together until stiff. Fold in the cooled angel's hair and almonds. Pile into the mould. If the biscuit palisade comes up too high, trim it off neatly, putting the cut ends over the top of the filling. Cover and chill at least 5 hours. Turn out to serve.

MALAKOFF/CHESTNUT CHARLOTTE

CHARLOTTE MALAKOFF/ST CLÉMENT

Why Malakoff? The pudding does have the look of a bulgy stockade. I imagine it was first made and named in the 1850s after the Malakoff tower at Sebastopol that the French took in the Crimean War, a victory glorious enough to celebrate.

Why St Clément? Not oranges and lemons for the French, but chestnuts, since he was the name saint of Clément Faugier, of Privas in the Ardèche. When the silk trade slumped in the nineteenth century, he commercialized a local delicacy, marrons glacés, to give people work. The firm produces chestnut purées as well, and prospers.

CHARLOTTE
2 packets boudoir biscuits
6 tablespoons rum or kirsch
24 lumps sugar

MALAKOFF
200 g (7 oz) almonds
250 g (8 oz) sugar
250 g (8 oz) unsalted French butter
pinch salt
3–4 tablespoons rum or kirsch
250 ml (8 oz) double cream

ST CLÉMENT
500 g (1 lb) can sweetened chestnut purée
100 g (3½ oz) unsalted butter
3–4 tablespoons rum or kirsch
300 ml (10 fl oz) double cream
bits of broken marrons glacés to decorate

Take a large pudding basin for the Malakoff, a charlotte mould for the St Clément. Put two strips of foil into the basin or mould, then line with the biscuits. Dip the base biscuits in the alcohol mixed with an equal amount of water. Make a caramel with the 24 sugar lumps. Dip the long side of each biscuit into the caramel before placing it against the sides, so that they are all glued together. Keep the sugar side out. Mix the remaining alcohol into the filling and put in the basin, with the remaining biscuits. Cover and leave overnight in the refrigerator. Turn out, after easing the charlotte by means of the foil straps. Decorate with toasted almonds or marrons glacés.

MALAKOFF Set aside a few almonds to blanch and toast for the final decoration, grind the rest unblanched not too finely. Beat sugar and butter, add almonds, salt and alcohol. Whip cream and fold in. Taste and add more alcohol if you like.

ST CLÉMENT Cream the butter, add purée and alcohol. Dilute any caramel remaining from the biscuits with a little very hot water, just enough to prevent it hardening, and mix with the cream. Whisk until firm. Put chestnut mixture into the biscuits first, then the cream.

NECTARINE BAVAROISE

Not a correct classic bavaroise, but a lighter mixture that allows the flavour of nectarine to come through particularly well. My original version, and the most successful, contained *orgeat*, an almond and orange-flower syrup tasting very much of the past that you can buy in high-class groceries and foodshops in France. Worth looking out for when you're on holiday. Kirsch can be used instead, or an orange-based liqueur.

Serves 6

6 nectarines,
approximately 375 g
(1½ lb)
125 g (4 oz) sugar
1 packet (½ oz) gelatine
juice of an orange
2 tablespoons orgeat or
appropriate alcohol

100 g (3½ oz) fromage
frais or yoghurt, drained
weight
100 ml (3½ fl oz) double
cream, whipped
lemon juice, see recipe

Into a wide shallow pan, section nectarines into eight wedges each. Sprinkle with the sugar and 2 tablespoons water. Cook on a low heat until the juices run, then raise the heat and finish the cooking. The red skins of the fruit will dye the syrup a glowing pink. Remove, drain and skin 12 sections. Put them in a whirligig star shape in the base of an oiled and sugared charlotte mould or other plain dish (use almond or a tasteless oil).

Put the rest of the fruit, skins and all, with the syrup into liquidizer or blender. Sprinkle on the gelatine, orange juice, and *orgeat* or alcohol. Whizz or process until very smooth. Strain into a basin, mix in the *fromage frais* or yoghurt, then fold in the cream. Taste and see if any lemon juice is needed to bring out the flavour. Add extra sugar if you like – icing sugar will mix in best at this stage, caster next best.

Carefully spoon some of the bavaroise over the nectarine sections in the dish, so as not to disturb them. Put in the coldest part of the refrigerator, or into the freezer, until almost set. Then spoon in the remaining mixture, starting round the edge so that it runs gently into the middle. Put back to set and chill.

To turn out, run a knife blade round the edge. Put a dish on top, then turn the whole thing over, and give a shake or two. If it is reluctant to turn out, put a cloth wrung out in very hot water over the metal mould, and shake again.

ICED PEAR SOUFFLÉ

SOUFFLÉ GLACÉ AUX POIRES

The lightest, whitest and most poetic of puddings, the best way of ending a special meal. It can be made with other fruit purées and an appropriate alcohol, or even gin if all else fails. Tiny mirabelle or cherry plums do very well: they should be lightly cooked like the pears, then sieved to get rid of stones and tough skin. Raspberries, strawberries, kiwi fruit, Cape gooseberries – in fact most soft fruit – need only be processed and then sieved if they have pips or stones. If this soufflé stands around, it can separate very slightly at the base. This does not matter, but it spoils the cloud-like appearance. Once you have made it, put it into the freezer, and aim to serve it in a frozen but soft condition, so that it is halfway between a fairly firm cold soufflé and an ice cream. If you have no freezer, and want to get ahead, make the Italian meringue up to 6 days in advance, and store it in a covered bowl in the refrigerator. Fruit and cream can be added a couple of hours beforehand, or less, and the whole thing returned to the cold.

Serves 6

250 g (8 oz) sugar
4 large egg whites
500 g (1 lb) Williams' or
Doyenné du Comice pears

1 lemon
300 ml (10 fl oz) double
cream
4 tablespoons pear eau de vie

First make the Italian meringue. Dissolve the sugar in 125 ml (4 fl oz) water over low heat. When clear, bring to the boil and boil hard until you reach the hard ball stage, 120°C (248°F). If the sugar crystallizes above syrup level, wash down the sides of the pan with a brush dipped in water.

Meanwhile whisk egg whites electrically. Pour on syrup straight from the stove, and continue whisking until the meringue swells to a cloudy mass. Or use a rotary beater.

Peel, core and chop pears coarsely. Cook with a tablespoon lemon juice until just tender. Process or crush to a smooth purée. Taste and add more lemon, but no sugar.

Fold whipped cream and *eau de vie* into the Italian meringue, then the fruit purée. Turn into a soufflé dish of a generous litre (2 pt) capacity, or a slightly smaller one collared with oiled paper. Serve chilled with almond biscuits.

PEACH OR NECTARINE SABAYON

Once you know how to make this most simple of sauces, you have a good basis for many puddings with soft fruit, either hot or cold. The obvious accompaniment is amaretto biscuits, but good macaroons do well instead.

Serves 4–6

4 large egg yolks
6 level tablespoons caster
sugar

4 tablespoons Amaretto di
Saronno
4 tablespoons orange juice

Put the ingredients into a large pudding basin or the top of a double boiler, and set over simmering water. Whisk steadily – you need an electric beater – until you have a light firmish cloud of a sauce, much increased in bulk from the original. It can be served warm at this point.

If you want to serve the sabayon cold, continue whisking for extra firmness, then remove the basin from the water and whisk until cold.

WARM PEACH SABAYON:
allowing 4 peaches for 6 people, slice into wedges, then halve them across. Warm them slightly to be of a similar temperature to the sauce, put them into a serving bowl and top with the sauce. Serve immediately.

GRATIN OF PEACHES:
allowing 6 peaches for 6 people, slice and arrange them over the base of a gratin dish, or 6 dishes. Pile on the sauce and brown

lightly under a hot grill. If the sauce has been made in advance and cooled, it is a good idea to reheat it gently over water, beating all the time, before piling it on the fruit.

SABAYON CREAM WITH PEACHES:

fold 6 tablespoons of whipped cream into the cold sauce. Put pieces of peach into 6 glasses, and pile the sauce on top. The cream lightens the sauce.

PASSION-FRUIT SOUFFLÉ

The appearance of passion fruit does not come up either to their name or their fragrance. They are the most humble-looking objects, sometimes yellowish green and plump, but most often in our markets at any rate a dark, wrinkled, purple-brown. Cinderellas of the fruit world. Inside it's another matter. The acid, sweet-smelling pulp – full of edible black seeds, hence the name of grenadilla or granadill, meaning 'little pomegranate' – can be eaten on its own, or be used to flavour creams, ices and soufflés. Or it can serve as a lemon, a tropical sort of lemon, to bring out the flavour of other fruits. Which, I think, makes it unique among exotic fruits. When buying passion fruit, choose the less wrinkled ones.

Serves 6

pulp and seeds of 8 passion fruit
juice of a small lemon
1 level dessertspoon gelatine

5 tablespoons water
150 g (5 oz) sugar
3 egg whites, beaten stiff

Mix passion-fruit pulp with the lemon juice. Stir gelatine, water and sugar over a low heat until you have a clear liquid. Add passion fruit and chill until set to the consistency of egg white.

Fold in the beaten egg whites and pour the mixture into a small soufflé dish, or 6–8 glasses. Chill to set.

SWEET PUMPKIN

HELVAEI KABAĞI KOMPOTOSU

Serve this brilliant, Turkish sweet dessert in tiny quantities. It has an Arabian Nights air to it.

Serves 8–10

1 kg (2 lb) slice of pumpkin
250 g (9 oz) sugar
approx. 125 g (4½ oz)
walnuts, chopped coarsely

225 g (8 oz) clotted cream,
or whipping or double
cream

Peel the pumpkin and remove the seeds and cottony part. Cut it into neat flat pieces.

Bring the sugar slowly to the boil with 150 ml (5 fl oz) water, stirring so that the sugar dissolves before boiling point is reached. Use a large, wide pan. Slip in the pumpkin pieces, which should lie more or less in a single layer. Simmer until they look transparent and tender. Cover the pan if the liquid disappears too fast, as the pumpkin should not be completely

candied, but very sweet and soft. This takes about 45 minutes.

Allow to cook and then put in 8–10 sundae glasses or small bowls. You may well have too much, but it freezes well. Scatter with just over half the walnuts. Serve well chilled and topped with clotted or whipped cream, and the last of the nuts.

Note: almonds, pistachios and hazelnuts may all be substituted for walnuts.

BURNT CREAM WITH CHINESE GOOSEBERRIES

CRÈME BRULÉE AUX KIWIS

Burnt cream has been made in England since the seventeenth century, but it gained a new reputation when a chef at Trinity College, Cambridge, took it up at the end of the last century. Being a rich pudding, it was usually served with fruit. Not long ago, someone had the idea of putting grapes underneath the pudding. And why not? Chinese gooseberries taste even better than grapes; so do Sharon persimmons which can be cut into slices and eaten while they are still firm (unlike other persimmons which have to be very soft). Raspberries and poached sliced peaches and pears do well, too.

The success of burnt cream depends partly on the flavour of the cream you use. Loseley or other farm brands or *crème fraîche* are ideal. Indeed, if you can buy one of them, and are in a hurry, you can use it whipped, instead of making custard.

Serves 10–12

about 375 g (1½ lb)
Chinese gooseberries
(kiwi fruit)
1 litre (1¾ pt) cream
thinly cut peel of a lemon

5 cm (2 in) cinnamon stick
4 large eggs
4 large egg yolks
sugar

Choose a large gratin dish that will hold 1½ litres (2½ pt) at least. Cover the base with peeled and sliced Chinese gooseberries.

Bring cream, peel and cinnamon slowly to just under boiling point. Strain on to eggs and yolks that have been beaten together in a large pudding basin: whisk together vigorously at first, then occasionally until you have a smooth cream. Put the basin over a pan of barely simmering water, and stir with a wooden spoon until very thick - the back of the spoon should be coated. Should the custard begin to show a hint of graininess, rapidly pour it into a processor or liquidizer and whizz at top speed for a few minutes. Pour over the fruit and chill for several hours.

A couple of hours before serving, sprinkle enough granulated sugar over the whole thing to make a ½ cm (scant ¼ in) depth. Preheat the grill to make it as red as possible. Slip the dish underneath. Do not turn your back on it, but be patient and watch as the sugar melts to a marbled brown glassiness. If the grill heat is uneven, you will have to turn the dish.

Some people stand the gratin dish in a tray of crushed ice before grilling the sugar. This is a good idea if your grill is not very hot, as it prevents the custard overheating underneath and bubbling up through the sugar. But I have never found it necessary.

STRAWBERRIES WITH ALMOND CREAM

Almonds have an affinity with fruit – almonds and raisins, almonds in apricot tarts, almonds and plums – but above all with strawberries. Almond biscuits are an obvious partner to strawberry fools and ices, for instance. And this almond cream to serve with strawberries makes a good change from double cream. It goes back to the almond milk of the Middle Ages, as far as the method goes. Try it with other fruit as well, apricots, peaches and pears, lightly poached in syrup.

Serves 6

5 heaped tablespoons almonds
½ litre (15 fl oz) whipping cream
caster sugar

German bitter almond essence, or Langdale's natural almond essence
generous 250 g (1–1¼ lb) hulled strawberries

Blanch and sliver a heaped tablespoon almonds. Spread them out on a baking sheet, and toast under a grill or in the oven. Set aside to cool.

Rinse and dry remaining almonds. If you have a blender or processor, reduce them to a sludge, skin and all, with 250 ml (8 fl oz) water. Otherwise grind them in a nut or electric mill.

Pour the cream into a wide shallow pan. Note the level. Stir in either the almond sludge or the ground almonds, plus the same quantity of water. Bring to boiling point and cook steadily – but do not let it boil over – until the level is the same or very slightly more than the original level of the cream. Put through a hair sieve or squeeze through a double muslin. Taste and add sugar. If the almond flavour needs bringing up, add a drop or two of essence, but do not overdo it.

Divide the strawberries between 6 glasses or small bowls. Sprinkle on a little sugar (this is better than oversweetening the cream). Let them stand awhile, until you are ready to serve the dish, then pour over the almond cream and scatter with the browned almonds. Do not chill.

Note: the almond debris can be incorporated into bread dough most successfully.

ELIZABETH RAFFALD'S ORANGE
CUSTARDS

Most of the best cookery books in this country have been written by women (or by foreigners). And of this energetic tribe, the most energetic of all was Elizabeth Raffald. Consider her career. She started work at fifteen, in 1748, ending up as housekeeper at Arley Hall in Cheshire. At thirty she married. Eighteen years later she was dead. During those eighteen years she organized: a cooked food shop selling pies, brawn, pickles, etc.; an enlarged cooked-food shop, with a confectionery department; the first domestic servants' employment agency; two important Manchester inns, or rather posting-houses; the first street and trade directory in Manchester (then a town of something over twenty thousand inhabitants); a couple of newspapers, as an *eminence rose*; an unreliable husband; fifteen (or sixteen – some conflict of evidence) daughters; and her cookery book, *The Experienced English Housekeeper*, published in 1769. Many of her recipes can be adapted to modern kitchen machines which she would thoroughly have approved of. She could always see the advantages of the latest thing, and add her own contribution to progress.

Serves 8–10

1 Seville orange
1 tablespoon brandy or
    orange liqueur
125 g (4 oz) caster sugar
2 eggs and 2 egg yolks

½ litre (16 fl oz) whipping
    cream
8–10 pieces candied orange
    peel

Simmer the rind of half the orange in water to cover for 15 minutes, or until fairly tender. Drain and liquidize or process to a smooth cream with alcohol, juice of the orange, sugar, eggs and yolks. Bring the cream to boiling point, then add gradually. Put in extra sugar, or a pinch of salt, if the flavour requires it.

Pour into 8 or 10 small soufflé dishes or custard cups or little cream pots (the kind with lids). Stand them in a roasting pan half full of very hot water, and put into the oven at Gas mark 2– 3, 150–160°C (300–325°F), for about 30 minutes until they are just set. At the lower temperature, they may need 35 minutes if the pots are deep rather than wide. Put a thin-bladed knife into one of the creams to test. If it comes out clean, or with a very slight creaminess, the custards are done (they will firm up as they cool, which you should bear in mind if you wish to serve them chilled). Take the pots of dishes from the water and, when cold, store overnight or several hours until chilled. Put a piece of candied orange peel in the centre of each one, and a tiny bay leaf if you have your own tree.

BANANA ICE CREAM

A mild but intriguing ice cream, set off by pieces of almond praline.

Serves 6

740 g (1½ lb) bananas
juice of a lemon
200 g (7 oz) sugar
1–2 tablespoons white rum
or kirsch
500–600 ml (15–20
fl oz) double or whipping
cream

ALMOND PRALINE
125 g (4 oz) unblanched
almonds
125 g (4 oz) sugar
4 tablespoons water

Peel, break up and process the bananas, or liquidize them, with the lemon juice. Dissolve the sugar in 200 ml (7 fl oz) of water over a low heat, bring to boiling point and boil hard for 3–5 minutes, until there is 300 ml (10 fl oz) syrup. Add to it 200 ml (7 fl oz) of cold water and add, with the rum or kirsch, to the banana.

Whip the cream until it is very thick but not stiff. Fold into the banana mixture carefully. Freeze in the usual way, with a sorbetière, ice bucket or freezer (page 78), following all the appropriate instructions.

To make the praline, put almonds and sugar into a heavy pan. Stir in the water, and heat gently so that the sugar melts. Raise the heat slightly so that the syrup gradually darkens to a caramel – stir from time to time. The nuts will pop when they are ready. Have a bowl of very cold water handy and stand the base of the pan into it to prevent the caramel going any darker. Spread the mixture out on to a greased metal sheet and leave it to cool and harden. When you serve the ice cream, scatter it with the praline, broken up into small pieces, not crumbs.

GINGER ICE CREAM

I think that ginger ice cream is very much a Christmas-time pudding, even a substitute for plum pudding. Those tubby porcelain and decorated jars of preserved ginger, often suspended by their rush lattice nets from the beams of old-fashioned grocery stores, are as much a sign of the season as tangerines and nuts. For those who are likely to suffer from too-much-ness, I offer a comforting thought from Dioscorides, the great Greek herbalist of the first century AD, who still influences some odd corners of our minds: he recommends ginger, for it has 'a warming, concocting power, mollifying of the belly gently, and good for the stomach'.

Serves 6–8

250 ml (8 fl oz) milk
2 egg yolks
1 egg
60 g (2 oz) ginger syrup
90–125 g (3–4 oz)
* preserved ginger, chopped*

250 ml (8 fl oz) double
* cream, whipped*
2 tablespoons icing or soft
* brown sugar*

Bring the milk to the boil and pour it on to the yolks and egg very gradually, beating the whole thing together (small wire whisks are the best for this kind of operation). Return to the pan and cook slowly over a low heat until the custard thickens: it must not boil or the egg will curdle. Immediately the thickness seems right, dip the base of the pan into a bowl of very cold water. This prevents the mixture continuing to cook in its own heat. Add the ginger syrup immediately after this, to hurry further the cooling process. If I sound fussy, I apologize, but even after 20 years' experience with custards things can go wrong, and one may as well minimize the risks.

Place this mixture in the freezing compartment of the refrigerator, which should be set at the coldest possible temperature. When it has set solid round the edges, remove it to a bowl, stir it up well and quickly incorporate the ginger pieces and whipped cream. Taste and add sugar gradually – ices should not be too sickly-sweet, mainly

on account of the flavour, but also because an oversweetened mixture freezes less well.

Return to the freezer and leave until hard. If the custard was frozen to the right amount before the ginger and cream was added, it should not be necessary to stir it at all during the second freezing process. If there was any doubt about this, stir it up gently after an hour, so that the ginger pieces do not sink to the bottom.

APPLE (OR PEAR) AND QUINCE
ICE CREAM

Water ice and whipped cream are the best ingredients for most soft fruit ice creams. For hard fruits such as apples and pears and quinces, or for dried fruits such as apricots and peaches, this is a good method.

250 g (8 oz) eating apples
  or pears or 375 g (12 oz)
  apples or pears
125 g (4 oz) quinces

60 g (2 oz) unsalted butter
2 tablespoons water
sugar to taste
2 eggs
150 ml (5 fl oz) each single
  and double cream
toasted almonds

Wash and cut up the fruit. Stew it slowly in a covered pan with the butter and water. Sieve to remove peel and cores. Flavour with sugar (if you are using apples alone add some apricot jam as well, or some cinnamon: with pears, lemon juice and a piece of cinnamon stick may be added as they stew). There should be about 300 ml (10 fl oz) of purée. Stir in the 2 egg yolks, beat well and reheat gently, keeping below the boil, for 5–10 minutes until the mixture thickens. Cool. Fold in the two creams, which should first be beaten together until thick, then freeze. When the mixture is almost solid, beat the egg whites and add spoonfuls of the frozen mixture until you have a thick frothy mass.

Refreeze. Serve garnished with toasted almonds.

The beaten whites are an optional addition, but they lighten the ice cream in a very agreeable way. It's worth making an effort to find a supply of quinces; they are a wonderful flavouring for apples and pears.

ICED GOOSEBERRY FOOL Substitute gooseberries for apples and quinces. Flavour with a muscatel dessert wine such as Frontignan. Or put a head of elderflowers in with the gooseberries as they stew. Serve with almond biscuits, and omit the garnish of toasted almonds.

FIGS IN SAUTERNES
WITH SAUTERNES AND ORANGE-FLOWER
ICE CREAM

From the Quady vineyard in California come rare bottles of a lovely dessert wine. Called Essencia, it's made from a variety of grape which has a hint of orange flowers in its muscat flavour. This gave me the idea of adding orange-flower water to Sauternes when making ice cream. Soon afterwards I came across a recipe, dating back at least 60 years, for making jelly from muscat grapes using Sauternes and orange-flower water. Foolish to think one can ever be original in cookery!

Serves 8

12 black or white figs
350g (12 oz) sugar
350 ml (12 fl oz)
  Sauternes (or another
  dessert wine)

ICE CREAM
300 ml (10 fl oz) milk
150 g (5 oz) sugar
6 egg yolks, beaten
600 ml (20 fl oz)
  whipping cream, beaten
  until very thick but not
  solid
175 ml (6 fl oz) Sauternes
1 teaspoon orange-flower
  water
2 tablespoons chopped
  pistachios to garnish

Rinse the figs and nip off the tough stem end. Put them stem end up in a pan into which they fit fairly closely. Put the sugar and wine to simmer with 350 ml (12 fl oz) water for 5 minutes. Pour over the figs and cook over a gentle heat until they are just tender – about 10 minutes, depending on ripeness. Remove from the heat and leave to cool. Halve the figs. Reduce the cooking liquor to a strongly flavoured syrup, about 225 ml (8 fl oz). Set both aside to chill.

For the ice cream bring the milk and sugar to the boil. Remove from pan and whisk into the egg yolks, then return to the pan and stir over a very low heat – a double boiler is best – to make a custard. Strain it into a bowl and leave to cool, stirring from time to time to prevent a skin forming. When barely tepid, fold the custard into the cream.

Now mix in the Sauternes gradually, tasting from time to time. Finally, add the orange-flower water. For me, these quantities are right, though you may like more orange-flower water. But go carefully: it can be a dominant flavour.

Freeze in an ice cream machine, following the manufacturer's instructions. Or put it into a freezer container and freeze for 1½–2 hours, or until almost set. Pour the mixture into a plastic bowl and beat so that it ends up with an even texture. Cover and put back into the freezer to firm. You can repeat the beating if wished.

Soften at room temperature for 15–20 minutes before serving. Spoon ice cream into 8 glasses, arrange 3 fig halves on top of each portion, tucking them in like petals, and scatter the centre with pistachio nuts. Pour a little of the syrup round the ice cream.

WILD APRICOT FOOL OR ICE CREAM

This is the best winter fool. Make an effort to find the small whole hunza apricots from Afghanistan. They have quite a different flavour from the usual kind, very spicy and delicate, yet the richness pervades the whipped cream.

Serves 4–6

175 (6 oz) wild dried apricots from Afghanistan (from Asian food shops and some health food shops) or 250 g (8 oz) apricots dried without sulphur dioxide (from better health food shops)

30 g (1 oz) blanched almonds
icing sugar
lemon juice
175 ml (6 fl oz) double cream
90–125 ml (3–4 fl oz) single cream

Soak the apricots, then simmer them in their soaking water for 5 minutes until just cooked, without adding sugar. Remove stones from the wild apricots, crack them and remove the kernels; crush the fruit with a fork and mix in the kernels. Otherwise, mash the ordinary dried apricots, and add the almonds, cut into slivers. Boil down the juice remaining from the fruit until it is syrupy and add that to the fruit. Sweeten with icing sugar, and add a little lemon juice to bring out the flavour.

Beat the creams together, and when stiff, fold in the fruit. Serve chilled, or frozen as an ice cream, with almond biscuits.

GRANITA AL CAFFÈ CON PANNA

On holiday in Italy in the heat, one rapidly discovers two surprising things – that *caffè espresso* is far more refreshing than water, or even a pink slice of water melon, and that bought ices can taste deliciously clear and subtle. These two bits of wisdom soon lead one to the finest of all water ices, *granita al caffè*, which combines the stimulus of black coffee with the refreshment of intense cold. And do not forget the important words *'con panna'* – with cream – because whipped cream sets off perfectly the bitter-sweet granules of blackish brown ice.

Use finely ground espresso coffee if you can buy it, otherwise a continental, after dinner roast.

Serves 6

12 slightly rounded tablespoons coffee

60–90 g (2–3 oz) sugar
1¼ litres (2 pt) water

Warm a stoneware jug, put in the coffee and then the water which should be boiling. Stir well and leave in a warm place for 10 minutes to brew. Strain off and sweeten with 60 g (2 oz) sugar. When cold, pour twice through a piece of sheeting or doubled muslin. Add more sugar if required. Freeze in the usual way, stirring every half hour until the mixture is a mush of granules.

Serve in tall glasses with a generous swirl of whipped cream on top.

GRAPE WATER ICE

Most fruit can be turned into a good sorbet or granita, but black grapes provide a flavour which is rich and subtle compared with the simpler flavours of orange or peach. Particularly when they are reinforced with a muscatel dessert wine, or brandy. White grapes produce a lighter-tasting ice of golden transparency – it will be improved by a white wine which has a pronounced grapey flavour.

Serves 6

500 g (1 lb) grapes
125 g (4 oz) sugar
150–300 ml (5–10 fl oz) water
juice of 1 lemon

3 tablespoons of dessert wine, or a glass of white wine, or a liqueur glass of brandy
1 or 2 egg whites (optional)

First produce a fruit purée. Cut the grapes in half and mangle them through a *mouli-légumes*, or liquidize for a few seconds. Make a syrup of the sugar and 150 ml (5 fl oz) water. When it is cool add the grape purée and strain. Flavour to taste with lemon juice. Dilute with the extra water if required.

Freeze in the usual way, stir-ring every half hour until the mixture is a mush of granules, adding the wine or brandy at the end. For instance with a granita, pour the wine in gradually at the last stirring; with a sorbet, add the wine when ice and beaten egg white are mixed together.

Serve with slightly sweetened whipped cream, and almond biscuits.

WINE SHERBET

Here is another superb water ice. To me it's the judgement of Paris, trying to decide between *granita al caffè* (page 81), this sherbet made with *muscat de Frontignan*, or black grape water ice (page 82. Champagne or sweet sparkling wine can be used as the flavouring for the syrup, but Frontignan, or a similar muscatel dessert wine, is a more economical choice as such wines do not spoil with a little keeping, once the bottle has been opened.

Serves 6

125 g (4 oz) sugar
300 ml (10 fl oz) (½ pt) wine

300 ml (10 fl oz) water
juice of 1 lemon
juice of 1 orange

Make a syrup of sugar and water by simmering for 5 minutes. Cool, then add the other ingredients and freeze to a granita (stirring every half hour until the mixture is a mush of granules). Serve in champagne flutes, with a topping of slightly sweetened whipped cream, and some almond or vanilla biscuits.

STRAWBERRY AND ORANGE ICE

Frozen strawberries can quite well be used for this recipe, which
makes a refreshing winter dessert.

Serves 6

250 g (8 oz) strawberries
60 g (2 oz) icing sugar
juice of 1 large orange
juice of 1 medium lemon
thinly-cut rind of 1
medium lemon

125 g (4 oz) granulated
sugar
2–3 tablespoons orange
liqueur or gin

Liquidize or process strawberries and icing sugar, then sieve to remove the seeds. Add citrus juices. Simmer rind, sugar and 300 ml (½ pt) water for 5 minutes.

Cool and strain gradually into the strawberry purée, tasting every so often to see if you have added enough (quantity will depend on flavour and sweetness of strawberries).

Freeze in the usual way: pour the mixture into a loaf tin and put into the freezer, or the ice-making part of the refrigerator set at its coldest. When the mixture is firm round the sides, stir sides to middle. When the mixture is consistently set but not hard, beat it well and add the alcohol. Make any adjustments of flavour. Whisk, with an electric beater for preference. Return to the freezer to set hard. Serve with almond biscuits.

KISSEL CUPS

Serves 6

230 g (8 oz) mixed
  blackcurrants
  and redcurrants
2 tablespoons clear honey
1 teaspoon grated orange
  zest
juice of 1 orange

15 g (½ oz) gelatine,
  soaked in 3 tablespoons
  cold water
110 g (4 oz) raspberries
110 g (4 oz) strawberries
3 tablespoons Grand
  Marnier

Place the currants in a pan with the honey, orange zest and juice. Bring to the boil, cover and simmer gently for 10 minutes. Add the soaked gelatine and stir until dissolved.

When cool, add the raspberries, strawberries and Grand Marnier, pour into 6 tumblers or ramekins and chill until set.

Serve, if you wish, with Greek yoghurt, or decorate with frosted currant leaves.

MANGO AND CARAMBOLA SALAD

Carambola (starfruit) makes the most delicious syrup for fruit salads, and you have the bonus of the starry shapes as well.

Serves 8

300 g (10 oz) sugar
2–3 carambola, sliced

3–4 fine ripe mangoes,
peeled, stoned and sliced
gin (optional)

Make a light syrup by dissolving the sugar in 600 ml (1 pt) of water over a low heat, with the ends of the carambola. Bring to the boil and boil steadily for 2 minutes. Slip in the star-shaped slices of carambola, lower the heat and simmer until they are tender (about 7 minutes). Remove the best stars for decoration. Taste the syrup and regard its consistency. If it needs to be more strongly flavoured and thicker, boil it down hard again. When you judge that it is about right, put in the mango and bring back to the boil. If the fruit is on the firm side, give it a minute or two's cooking; if it is juicy and just right, remove the pan from the heat when it returns to the boil. The idea is to impregnate the mango with some of the acidity, not to cook it in the accepted sense.

Arrange the mango slices in a shallow dish with the stars of carambola you set aside. Taste the syrup as it cools down and decide whether a little gin would give it an agreeable lift. If so, add it by the tablespoonful. Gin is a splendid spirit with fruit, sometimes to be preferred to kirsch.

Strain the syrup over the mango, being careful not to drown it. Remaining syrup can be stored in the refrigerator for other salads.

Note: ripe orange-fleshed melon can be substituted for mango. With pears, be prepared to cook them a little longer. In a mixed fruit salad – be discreet with the mixture – some of the fruits will not need cooking or heating at all, for example lychees.

ORANGE SALAD WITH ORANGE THINS

This salad could be served with a chocolate cake, on its own, or as
the only dessert, accompanied by orange thins.

Serves 8

14–16 oranges, well
  scrubbed
4 pomegranates
icing sugar
orange-flower water

BISCUITS
250 g (8 oz) softened butter
250 g (8 oz) caster sugar
  from vanilla pod jar
1 large egg
1 tablespoon double cream
300 g (10 oz) plain flour
¼ teaspoon salt
1 teaspoon baking powder
grated zest of 1 orange and
  1–2 tablespoons juice (see
  recipe)

Remove the orange zest of as many of the oranges as you feel inclined: use a zester for the thinnest, most delicate shreds, or else peel off thin strips with a peeler, cut them into shreds and blanch until tender for a minute or so in boiling water. Set aside the zest of 1 orange and, as you work, 1–2 tablespoons of juice for the biscuits. Keep the rest of the shreds for the salad.

Peel the oranges to the quick, then slice them tidily across. Discard – i.e. eat – the ends, then arrange the slices in concentric circles on a dish, the lines alternating in direction. Leave a space in the centre. Remove pips as you go.

Roll the pomegranates on a firm surface to loosen the insides, then cut through the skins, open them up and scoop out the seeds, avoiding the bitter yellow part. Pile them in the centre of the oranges with their juice. Sprinkle lightly with icing sugar and a little orange-flower water. To make the biscuits, make a dough with all the ingredients, having first sifted the flour, salt and baking powder. Scoop on to a piece of baking parchment and form into a smooth cylinder. Then flatten it so that when it comes to be sliced, you will have cat's tongue ovals.

Wrap in the parchment and chill until firm, or, if made in advance, freeze until required.

Slice off thinly as many biscuits as you require and place on a baking sheet lined with parchment. Bake in an oven preheated to gas 5, 190°C (375°F) for about 10 minutes. Put the remaining dough back in the fridge or freezer for another time.

Serve the salad at room temperature rather than chilled, accompanied by the biscuits.

COMPOTE OF PEARS WITH QUINCE AND VANILLA

A beautiful red dish for autumn dinners, the colour set off by the bloomy blackness of a vanilla pod. Not much good my giving advice on choosing quinces. You have to buy what you can find, and be thankful. Like the mulberry, the quince is a tree to look out for in other people's gardens in case they are willing to share its fruit.

Serves 6

4 quinces
1 whole vanilla pod

250 g (8 oz) sugar
8 large pears

Rub any grey fluff from the quinces. Wash them and remove peel, then quarter and core them. Put the vanilla pod and quince debris into a pan and cover generously with boiling water. Simmer steadily for half an hour, covered. Strain off the liquid into another pan, extricate the vanilla pod from the quince debris, and put it into the pan with the liquid, plus the sliced quince and sugar. Simmer with a lid on the pan, until the fruit begins to become tender and the liquid looks deep pink. Peel and core the pears, cutting them into wedges. Put them carefully into the pan, cover and leave to simmer until the pear slices are tender.

Remove the fruit to a bowl with a slotted spoon. Taste and consider the liquid: if it is copious and watery, boil it down hard. It should have a syrupy consistency. Pour over the fruit, putting the pod on top, and leave to chill. Serve with cream and little biscuits: shortbreads or almond biscuits are the best kind.

INDEX

Index